Redford Township District Library
25320 West Six Mile Road
Redford, MI 48240

www.redford.lib.mi.us

Hours:

Mon–Thur 10–8:30
Fri–Sat 10–5
Sunday (School Year) 12–5

94

9763725

18.95

THE GREAT IRON LINK
The Building of the Central Pacific Railroad

Great Events

THE GREAT IRON LINK
The Building of the Central Pacific Railroad

Rosemary Laughlin

MORGAN
REYNOLDS
Incorporated

Greensboro

THE GREAT IRON LINK *The Building of the Central Pacific Railroad*

Library of Congress Cataloging-in-Publication Data
Laughlin, Rosemary
  The great iron link : the building of the Central Pacific Railroad / Rosemary Laughlin.
— 1st ed.
     p. cm. — (Great events)
  Includes bibliographical references and index.
  Summary: Recounts the building of the Central Pacific Railroad and sketches the lives of
the five meN whose idea it was: Theodore Judah, Charlie Crocker, Leland Stanford, Mark
Hopkins, and Collis Huntington.
  ISBN 1-883846-14-5 (hardcover)
     1. Central Pacific Railroad Company—Juvenile literature. [1. Central Pacific Railroad
Company. 2. Railroads.]   I. Title II. Series
TF25. C4L38 1996
385'. 0979—dc20

                                                              96-21722
                                                                  CIP
                                                                  AC

Photo on pages 80-81courtesy of the Oakland Museum of California. All other photos and
maps courtesy of the Stanford University Archives.

Printed in the United States of America
First Edition

Contents

Chapter One

To California

On Christmas Day of 1830 the locomotive *Best Friend of Charleston* completed a six-mile trip over the Charleston and Hamburg rail line. This was the first successful passenger railroad in America. Over the next thirty years, many people dreamed of building a railroad across the continent. At first the idea seemed so crazy that the advocates of a transcontinental railroad, fearing ridicule, were afraid to make their ideas public. Skeptics seemed to have the stronger argument. How could such a great distance ever be spanned with wooden ties and iron rails?

But the stubborn dreamers kept the idea alive until, in the dark years of the Civil War, construction on the giant project began. The building of the transcontinetal railroad was carried out by two companies. One company, the Union Pacific, built west from Omaha, Nebraska. The Central Pacific built east from San Francisco, across the forbidding Sierra Nevada mountain range. The Central Pacific was created by five men. Theodore Judah, Charlie Crocker, Mark Hopkins, Leland Stanford, and Collis Huntington were different from one another in many ways. But fate, and their ability to seize an opportunity, brought the five together and they, along with the labor of hundreds of men and women, helped to make the dream of a transcontinental railroad come true.

After the railroad was completed, four of the five men became wealthy and powerful enough to have a stranglehold on the economic well-being of the entire country. The controversy that developed over the Big Four's monopoly raised questions about the role of individual and corporate power that are still hotly debated today.

The building of the Central Pacific railroad is also the story of the thousands of laborers who built the road, especially the Chinese and immigrant Irish workers, whose strong backs were as critical to the railroad construction as the money and business acumen of their bosses.

This book tells the story of the Central Pacific and how it changed the country. But before the railroad could be built, five men had to make their way to California from the Northeast.

Theodore Judah

Twelve-year-old Ted Judah's heart pounded as he listened to Professor Amos Eaton describe how railroads would change the future. Professor Eaton, who was developing the first curriculum in the United States for a professional degree in Civil Engineering at the Rensselaer Polytechnic Institute, allowed the students to discuss their studies on the front porch of the school building. Upperclassmen sat in rocking chairs; younger students, like Ted Judah, sat on the floor.

The double-headed locomotive *South Carolina* ran on the Charleston-Hamburg line

"Railroads will shape the destiny of our great country," Eaton exclaimed. "But first civil engineers must create locomotives and tracks that are safe and efficient. We must have boilers that do not explode. We must have tracks that do not spring up and pierce the cars. We must have roadbeds that do not heave with changing temperatures. We must have better warnings of a train's approach than trumpets and megaphones. We must develop lighting so trains can travel by night. We must build safe bridges and trestles and fills. I intend to assign some of you to work with the survey crews on the new rail lines. You will see the problems. Then you can solve them with what you know from your studies."

Suddenly, Professor Eaton's lecture was disrupted by the

clanking wheels and piercing whistle of an approaching train. The boys jumped up to clear the school's geese and cows from the tracks. As the boys waved their coats and yelled "Git! Git!" at the retreating animals, the train engineer waved gratefully. The five-car, three-ton train huffed on across the New York countryside at the amazing speed of twenty miles per hour.

Ted's father had cast a spell over him with stories of how railroads would open the West, helping the United States to fulfill its destiny of someday stretching from coast to coast. His father was dead now. Ted missed him so much. His stories had become Ted's dreams, and he was determined to play a role in bringing the railroads to the West.

In the summer of 1839, after his thirteenth birthday, Ted made an important decision. His mother could no longer afford to pay his tuition at engineering school. She wanted Ted to join the Navy.

Ted, however, accepted a job as a surveyor's assistant on the Schenectady and Troy Railroad. Today we might describe this work as being a "gofer"—to "go for" the equipment the surveyor needed, especially the chains used to mark the measurements.

Ted did his job so well that he was praised by the foreman, Sidney Dillon. When Dillon launched his own business as a railroad contractor, he hired young Ted as a surveyor. Later, he promoted Ted to assistant civil engineer. Dillon's business made money. Between 1841 and 1846 his company built new lines criss-crossing Massachusetts and Vermont. By this time, many of the problems Professor Eaton had called his students'

Theodore Judah was familar with the Dewitt Clinton locomotive that ran on the Albany & Schenectady line.

attention to had been solved. Railroads brought progress. Enterprising citizens wanted them in their towns.

During 1843 and 1844, Ted surveyed on the line going up the Connecticut River Valley from Springfield, Massachusetts to Brattleboro, Vermont. One Sunday he rode into Greenfield, Massachusetts to attend Sunday services at St. James Episcopal Church. Dressed in his best clothes, with a neatly trimmed beard, dark-eyed Ted was a handsome figure. His velvet vest with polished brass buttons and his erect bearing caught people's eye.

After the service, the parishioners welcomed Ted. Among the welcomers was a gray-eyed young lady with red glints in her brown hair. When Ted was introduced to Anna Pierce the two felt a magnetic attraction.

Anna and Ted were married on May 10, 1847. Shortly before the wedding, Ted did something daring. He had heard engineers say that it was impossible to build a railroad in the narrow Niagara River Gorge, although one was badly needed to connect the ship piers of Lake Erie and Lake Ontario. Ted made a trip to the gorge and surveyed. He double checked his figures. Then he made an appointment with some prominent businessmen. He presented them with a proposal: "Gentlemen, raise the money and I will build your railroad." They were astounded, and more than a little skeptical, but soon were convinced by this young man who backed everything he claimed with data. They hired him.

Ted oversaw the work in the rocky narrow gorge. An accomplished artist, Anna spent her time painting one of

America's most romantic landscapes. She painted their red cottage high on the cliff, with the pretty little gazebo and the hairpin road leading to it. In the background roared the panoramic falls. A boat steamed towards the falls. The railroad bed wound along the Niagara River.

When the Niagara Gorge Railroad was finished, the Judahs moved to Buffalo. One March day in 1854, Governor Horatio Seymour of New York received a visitor. Colonel Charles Wilson had followed the Gold Rush to California in 1849, but ended up operating a store on a boat that steamed up and down the Sacramento River. Excited miners with gold in their pockets were willing to pay high prices for his goods. Next, Colonel Wilson built toll roads near San Francisco.

Farther east, Colonel Wilson had seen wagons slowly hauling men and freight back and forth from the mines in the mountains. Now he wanted a railroad that would connect foothill towns with the growing city of Sacramento. Eventually, he hoped to extend his rails. He had come to New York City, the railroad center of the United States, to get a good builder.

"I know a young civil engineer, just the right man for you," said Governor Seymour. "His name is Theodore Dehone Judah. If you can get him. He's been in high demand since his triumph in the Niagara Gorge."

The men telegraphed Ted in Buffalo: "Come to New York City at once on business."

Ted was excited. "I am going to New York City on tonight's train," he told Anna. "I must respond to a call from such men, though I don't know what's up." Three days later she received a telegram from Ted. "Home tonight. We sail for California on April 2nd."

Anna knew this opportunity meant everything to Ted. She had seen him read and study about the possibility of a continental railroad. Many times he had said, "It *will* be built, and I am going to have something to do with it." Their friends had laughed and said he was just building castles in the air. Anna understood his vision.

What Ted wanted, Anna wanted. His telegram had read, "*We* sail for California April 2nd." It showed how they understood each other. He had already booked passage.

The Judahs sailed to California on a ship owned by Cornelius Vanderbilt. The voyage took them to Nicaragua, and up the San Juan River to Lake Nicaragua, where they transferred to a coach that took them over the mountains to the Pacific coast where a ship awaited to take them north to San Francisco.

Ted was busy every minute of the journey. When he wasn't examining the ship and talking to the crew and the other California-bound passengers, he was poring over his California maps.

The Judahs' arrival in San Francisco was exhilarating. Colonel Wilson met them on the sunny, windy day. He took them to a special lunch, where Judah announced he wanted to begin work on the Sacramento Valley Railroad the next day. Soon they were on their way to Sacramento—75 miles as the crow flies, but 150 miles via the twisting Sacramento River.

Charlie Crocker

"Goodbye-e-e! So lo-o-ng. God keep you-u!"

Twelve-year-old Charlie Crocker, his mother, and sister, called their farewells. Charlie's father and four brothers were off to Indiana. The year was 1834.

Charlie watched the men float out of sight down the Erie Canal. The boat they were on was pulled by mules that walked on a path along the bank. Charlie wished he was going with them. But his father had decided otherwise. He wanted Charlie to stay behind and help his mother.

It wasn't long before Mrs. Crocker discovered that the money her husband had left behind wasn't going to last. Charlie, who already had a job hawking newspapers, decided he could become an agent, which meant he would hire others to work for him. Becoming an agent meant he would have to quit school and borrow $200 to purchase the exclusive right to sell papers on the Hudson River Ferry. But he was certain he could turn a profit.

Mrs. Crocker did not like to see Charlie quit school, but she knew he was sharp about money and was willing to work.

Soon the streets of Troy, New York were filled with the loud voice of Charlie Crocker as he bellowed the name of the paper and the headlines and yelled at other newsboys attempting to invade his territory. Sometimes his loud voice wasn't enough and he had to fight to protect his franchise. It kept him busy. One day when he had a cold, his mother urged him to stay home. He replied, "I have no nursery days. I can work day and night."

Things did not move as smoothly in Indiana as Mr. Crocker had thought. He had a farm, but lacked the money to send for Charlie, his sister and mother. Charlie yearned to see the new country. He had made enough money for the trip, so off they went to Indiana in 1836.

Soon after his arrival Charlie was working long, hard days on the farm with his brothers. They had to clear the land by chopping trees and removing their roots before they could plow and plant. Charlie had been his own boss in Troy. Now he felt like a slave. At seventeen, Charlie could stand it no more. When his father told him he would never be a good farmer, Charlie knew he'd had enough of the farm life.

Charlie began working for himself again, saving money for eight years. He worked for other farmers and at a sawmill. He built and ran an iron foundry. Along the way he fell in love with Mary Deming, the sawmill owner's daughter.

When gold was discovered in California in 1848, everyone wanted to go and make a fortune. Charlie was no different. He and a brother set out with a wagon train. Soon Charlie was the leader. He explained later, "They would all gather around me and want to know what to do....I was always the one to swim a river and carry the rope across." When wagons broke down, Charlie knew how to fix them. Charlie loved the outdoors and the hard travel.

Charlie arrived in California in April 1850, but he did not find gold. This did not discourage him. "I was always apt at trade," he said, and he started a hardware store with his brother in a mining camp. Later, they moved it to Sacramento. In

November, 1852, he returned to Indiana to marry Mary Deming. The newlyweds decided to return to California by sea. It took six weeks to sail from New York to Panama, to cross overland to the Pacific Ocean, and to board another ship to San Francisco, where they switched to a boat that took them sixty-five miles up the winding Sacramento River.

Mark Hopkins

"Well, boys, what was Father's sermon about?" Mrs. Hopkins had a new baby and was unable to go to church services this Sunday morning in the mid-1820s in Henderson, New York.

Mark had paid attention to the sermon. It was about the Parable of the Talents in the gospel of Matthew. The moral was that God expected you to do good with whatever ability you had, just as the master in the story expected his servants to multiply the money he had given each when he left.

Mark wondered about his "talents." It was clear that his brother Moses's talent was to have a good time and to make people laugh. But Mark was not like Moses. He was smart and quiet and liked to listen to other people's ideas and plans.

All his life, Mark Hopkins would keep these characteristics. He was soft spoken, kind, loved animals, and spent time caring for the family's horses and dogs. He was good at school, particularly in math. He kept his books and papers neat. His beautiful handwriting was never mussed with ink blots, and it was always perfectly clear to read. Physically, he was thin, and his face always looked a little sad. He spoke with a lisp.

In 1828, when Mark was fifteen, his father died. Mark had to quit school to help his two older brothers run their store. After a while, he became a law clerk in Niagara, New York. In those days, most men did not go to law school. They learned by working for a lawyer and studying his books. When they felt they were ready to pass the bar by taking a test, they did so. Mark Hopkins passed, but soon realized it was the knowledge of the law and not the practice of it that he liked.

Mark took a job as a bookkeeper in New York City. However, he had enough restlessness to be struck with the gold fever that came sweeping in from California in 1848. He was thirty-five years old, and wanted to try his luck. He did something very daring and uncharacteristic for him. He joined a group of twenty-five other "Forty-niners" as they were called. Each one put $500 into a pool to buy mining equipment.

Mark Hopkins' passage to California was a frightening experience. Because the group had so much heavy mining equipment, they had to take the long way to California by boat around Cape Horn at the tip of South America. It was a voyage of 17,000 miles, and it took 196 days—from January to August. It was an awful trip with terrible storms, seasickness, a mean captain, bad food, and rationed water. Hopkins' group found themselves in a quarrelsome mood when they finally reached San Francisco. They could not agree what to do, so they split up their supplies and went their separate ways.

Hopkins and four others bought two wooden boats and slowly rowed their way against the current up the Sacramento River toward the Sierra Nevada Mountains. It was miserably

Horse-drawn boats provided transportation on the Erie Canal before the coming of the railroads.

hot, and the rowing was grueling work. When they could go no further by water, they traded their boats for two wagons and two tired oxen to pull them. As they moved slowly along, they met discouraged miners returning empty handed. Winter was coming on, and Hopkins and his partners felt as worn-out as their oxen.

Leland Stanford

Josiah Stanford was a man of action. In 1832, when his son Leland was six, a railroad was built from Albany to Schenectady, New York. The new road was called the Mohawk and Hudson and Josiah decided to sell his tavern on the Watervliet Wharf of the Erie Canal and move closer to the new railroad. There would be plenty of trees there that could be chopped down and used to build a new tavern.

Little Leland tried to picture his father's words. There were few trees around the Erie Canal, although he could see them on the distant hills up the Hudson River Valley. The words *forest* and *woods* popped up in the stories his mother read to him.

But Leland and his six brothers soon understood what it meant to chop down trees, for Josiah meant to supply the new railroad with wood to be used as fuel by the locomotives. The elms, beeches, maples, and pines fell to their sharp axes to be split into the right-sized logs for the firemen to handle. The Stanford property was a perfect re-fueling spot for trains, located halfway between Albany and Schenectady, at the base of long grades to the river bluffs at each end.

The Stanfords chopped more wood than the railroad needed and Leland was sent into Albany to peddle it. He avoided driving past the store of Dyer Lathrop, because he did not want to be seen in country-boy clothes by Lathrop's daughter, Jane.

Energetic Josiah was not one to let any opportunities go untried. He and his boys did construction work for the Mohawk and Hudson. He farmed in order to supply food to his inn.

Leland as a teenager was big and plain-looking. He was quiet, responding slowly and speaking deliberately. He loved to read, especially biographies of men like George Washington, Benjamin Franklin, and Francis Marion. Josiah perceived him as evidence of the proverb, "Still waters run deep." Josiah wanted Leland to have a good education and enrolled him, in 1841, at a school near Utica, and later at the Cazenovia Methodist Seminary near Syracuse.

After graduation, Leland went to an Albany law office where he would get the practical knowledge he needed to become a lawyer. No longer in outdoor work-clothes, he revived his acquaintance with Jane Lathrop and courted her. They were engaged in 1848, after he was admitted to the bar.

Leland Stanford did what many new doctors, lawyers, and schoolteachers did. He moved west to start a law practice. He chose Port Washington, Wisconsin, north of Milwaukee on Lake Michigan. In 1850, he married Jane and took her to Wisconsin. His brothers, however, went all the way to California after gold was discovered. When a fire destroyed Leland's office, and the Port Washington business district, in 1852, he decided to join his brothers in California. His eldest brother had a successful grocery business in Sacramento, and had set up branch stores in the small mining towns in the hills. Stanford would manage one of them, but he did not want Jane to live in a rough mountain town. Jane's father was ill, so nursing him in Albany was another reason for her to stay behind until he found a suitable home. After her husband was gone, Jane heard that people were gossiping that her husband had deserted her.

Leland returned to Albany after receiving news that Jane's father had died. Jane now viewed California as an escape from the cruel Albany gossip. The couple traveled west by ship, via Panama. Jane was miserably sea-sick. Her husband comforted her, saying, "I will build a railroad one of these days for you to go back on."

Collis Huntington

When thirteen-year-old Collis Huntington returned from school to the cottage in Poverty Hollow, near Harwinton, Connecticut in 1834 and saw his mother crying, he knew there could only be one reason for her distress. His father had left again.

Collis glanced at the tool shed. The door hung open. The tools were gone. The pattern was familiar. When everything was broken, and farming was unpleasant, Mr. Huntington took off to mend pots and pans until he had enough money to patch things up. He never went beyond patching. The cottage was crowded with six children. Clothes were the same old hand-me-downs. The children seemed never to get their fill of food.

After his father left, several of the selectmen from the Harwinton town council visited. They had found two farmers willing to pay Collis and his brother, Solon, seven dollars a month and food and clothes for work. The two boys would have to agree to work on the farms for a year.

This arrangement turned out very well for Collis. He worked for Orson Barber, and they got along well. In the evenings Mrs. Barber taught Collis history, including Ben Franklin's story. If one were smart enough and willing to work hard, prosperity would follow, she said. *Thrift* was the key. *Waste not, want not.* These ideas were definitely valued by most people in rural Connecticut.

Collis practiced thrift. At the end of his year at the Barbers, he had not spent one penny of the $84 he had earned. He had no desire to go back home and be under his father's incompetent rule again, so he began working for another neighbor who ran a little store.

Collis amazed the storekeeper by memorizing the cost of every item in stock. He knew both wholesale and retail prices and calculated the profits in his head. Soon he was being sent out as a peddler. On one trip Collis met the Stoddard family and was charmed by one of their very nice girls, Elizabeth.

By age sixteen, Collis had gained the confidence to strike out on his own. He had saved $175. With it, and two letters of character recommendation, he went by himself to New York City to buy goods and a peddler's wagon for long-range selling trips. He looked much older than he was, with his large six-foot frame and strong, muscular body.

For the next few years Collis was one of the "Yankee peddlers," who moved through rural America before the Civil War. He also collected debts for a fee. One look at Collis' size and strength convinced most debtors that they didn't want to hold back their money any longer. In the summer, Collis ranged as far west as Indiana; in the winter he went South. He liked people, but he also did not mind being alone at night with a book to read, sleeping outdoors with his horse and wagon. He made money, and he kept his mind open for new and better opportunities. He did not want to be a peddler all his life.

In 1841, Collis went to visit his brother Solon in Oneonta, New York. Solon had just built a beautiful stone store, and he offered Collis a job. Solon made him a partner in less than two years. Then Collis rushed to Connecticut to court Elizabeth Stoddard. They were married September 18, 1844, and moved to a nice little house in Oneonta. They were happy, for Collis liked the exercise provided by house chores such as chopping wood, and he enjoyed Elizabeth's company after work. He was never one to spend time or money in taverns, as many men did. He was also the one who went to New York City to sell local produce.

In 1848, when gold was discovered at Sutter's Mill east of Sacramento, not even sober New Englanders were immune to the gold-fever that swept the country. Collis and Solon were cautious, however. They thought the reports of vast amounts of gold were exaggerated, and that as hordes of men invaded California, the chances of making an easy fortune would lessen. However, the gold-seekers would have to eat, wear clothes, and find shelter. They would need mining supplies. Collis would go to California and scout out the opportunities. Solon would stay and ship whatever goods Collis found profitable. On his first trip, Collis loaded up woolen socks, rifles, and all-purpose medicine.

Collis teamed up with five other men from Oneonta. On March 15, 1849, the Oneonta group sailed from New York City on the paddle-wheel steamer *Crescent City* for Panama.

Seasickness was the only problem on the first leg of the trip, which lasted nine days. Then the real unpleasantness began. The Panama isthmus (this was before the building of the Panama Canal) was forty-seven miles wide. In 1849, passengers were on their own once the steamer unloaded them and their baggage on the Atlantic coast.

The travelers hired natives in dugout boats, called *bongos,* to take them twenty-three miles up the Chagres River to Gorgona; a three day trip through the dark, steamy jungle. Movement against the strong current was done by poling. Most of the passengers preferred to sleep in the *bongos* at night rather than on the muddy river banks. The mosquitoes were terrible and fever and disease took many lives.

At Gorgona, the men transferred to mules for the remaining twenty-four mile ride. Once in Panama City, they awaited ships coming up from the route around Cape Horn or those shuttling between Panama and San Francisco. Waiting was not pleasant. There were few decent hotels in Panama City, and most passengers chose to live in tents outside the city walls. Conditions were unsanitary. If people ate local fresh fruit they got dysentery, a disease that can lead to fatal loss of body liquids. The tropical climate dumped rain on them; mold burst and crawled like slow fire. More travelers arrived each day to swell the numbers. They worried not only about avoiding malaria and cholera, but also about getting on the next boat. One boat could not possibly take them all. Would first arrivals get to go, or those who would pay the most?

When Huntington and the passengers from *Crescent City* arrived in Panama City, they learned they had just missed a ship departing for San Francisco. They would have to wait six weeks. Some of the men passed the time gambling and drinking. Collis concentrated on taking advantage of his misfortune. On the mule ride in he had noticed sunny clearings with working ranches. He thought he might be able to buy what those ranches produced and sell the goods to the people in Panama City.

Huntington put on a huge Panama hat to protect him from the blazing sun and set out on foot back towards Gorgona. He found that staple foods were grown on the ranches, and that mats and cool cloth were woven. The ranchers were willing to sell. Collis carried his money in a belt at his waist. He bargained, then hired mules for transport. He sold everything at a profit and went back for more. He did this at least twelve times, never once getting sick.

On one trip he heard of a river schooner for sale. He investigated, bought it, hired several natives for crew, and loaded it with supplies to sell along the Pacific coast. He had arrived in Panama with $1200 in his money belt and departed with $5000.

The last leg of the voyage was eventful, too. Not everyone could get aboard the first steamship that arrived. Amidst the shouting and milling around the ticket office, the boom of a cannon announced a second arrival. Still, there were more passengers than spaces. Amazingly, a third ship, the *Humboldt*, appeared; it had no steam engine, only sails. Its owners were on board, and when they saw how many people wanted passage, they ordered the crew to make as many narrow bunks as they could. When the travelers came aboard and realized how unsafe the crowding had made the ship, they cornered the owners and ordered them to remove some passengers by lot. The owners refused.

Who knows what would have happened had not a fourth ship arrived? Over eighty travelers transferred to it. The *Humboldt's* fare was cheaper, and Huntington chose to stay aboard. He soon regretted his decision. The steamships arrived in San Francisco in May, but the *Humboldt* was becalmed by lack of wind for five weeks. The passengers stared at beautiful sunsets and became hungrier and thirstier. Weevily biscuits and stale beans were rationed. Fights broke out. In late June the winds finally came, followed by rain that replenished their water supply.

Finally, on August 30th, the *Humboldt* made its way through the fog into San Francisco Bay. The experience had been so terrible that some years later the survivors began to have reunions each August 30th to celebrate their ordeal. Huntington always attended. The survival of that trip was a triumph and symbol to them for the rest of their lives.

Chapter Two

The Businessmen Get Started

When Charlie and Mary Crocker disembarked from the riverboat, they discovered that their hardware store had burned to the ground in a fire that had swept through Sacramento's business district. Fortunately, Crocker had brought new goods with him from the East, and soon his happy voice was bellowing from behind a new counter.

One of the big topics of conversation in Crocker's store was the new Republican Party. Crocker liked its anti-slavery position, and its concern for extending the railroad across the country to California. Crocker was elected city alderman. While serving on the city council he met another hardware store owner, Mark Hopkins. Hopkins was also a Republican, but he was as thin, wispy, and soft-voiced as Crocker was big, loud, and bossy.

In 1857, Crocker ran for the California Assembly. He was on the Republican ticket with a grocer from Sacramento named Leland Stanford. Both were defeated. Crocker did not feel disappointed for long. His restless eye looked for something new and exciting.

Mark Hopkins had made a decision shortly before he met Crocker. He had not found gold in the mountains. He gave up mining, returned to Sacramento, and invested what little money he had left in more supplies. In the cold, rainy weather, he took these out to the miners in the hills. But the miners were discouraged and had little money. Fortunately, he met a shipboard acquaintance whom he had liked. The two men pooled what they had and opened a store in Sacramento. This store prospered until it was destroyed by the same fire that destroyed Charlie Crocker's.

By 1854, Mark Hopkins was forty-one, and the restlessness that had brought him to California was gone. He knew what it was like to take risks. He knew what it was like to lose. He knew that one had to give up dreams when they became foolish. He also knew that he wanted to settle in California for good.

Hopkins had been writing to his cousin Mary Frances Sherwood in New York. He missed her. When he returned to New York on a buying trip, he asked her to marry him. Mary said yes. She loved to read romantic novels of adventures and happy endings in marriage. California held all sorts of glamorous possibilities, even for a woman as old as she—thirty-six.

Leland Stanford worked hard after arriving in California. He took over the Sacramento store so that his brothers Josiah and Philip could open another store in San Francisco. When two customers who owed Stanford money offered him stock in their quartz mine as payment he took the stock. Others had thought the mine worthless, but it soon became wildly productive and made a great deal of money.

With his business affairs doing well, Stanford built a home for Jane, who was warmly welcomed in Sacramento society. He became involved in civic affairs and politics, and helped establish the new Republican Party in California. He felt it took stronger anti-slavery positions than did the old parties.

Upon his arrival in San Francisco in August, 1849, Collis Huntington stored his goods in a tent town on the beach and looked for ways to get nearer to the mines. He found a river steamer being loaded by a single man. It was bound for Sacramento. Huntington offered his help in loading and unloading in exchange for hauling his goods.

Huntington settled in Sacramento. He suffered setbacks from the same fires and floods and high freight charges as the others, but was always able to pick up and re-start. He paid his bills and tricked no one with bad merchandise. He did not gamble or participate in any way in the roughness of the West. After a year, he returned East to bring Elizabeth to Sacramento.

By 1854, Huntington had met Mark Hopkins and the two became partners in an hardware store. Both men were thrifty. Hopkins stayed at the store, while Huntington searched for bargains. He went regularly to San Francisco to scout the warehouses, and to watch for the black arms of the signal tower on Telegraph Hill that announced a ship's arrival. When they flipped up, Huntington hurried to an old rowboat harbored at Clark's Point and was usually the first to approach the ship and ask about the cargo. If it contained something he wanted, he

Collis Huntington seized on every opportunity to make a profit.

would buy it and arrange for transfer to a Sacramento-bound steamer.

Huntington and Hopkins's basic business principle was simply stated: "Anything that can be bought for less than production, is not perishable, and is an article in use is worth buying and holding." The two men set up storage tents and built warehouses. The town storytellers enjoyed spreading stories of Huntington's shrewdness. One story was about the blasting powder he bought and stored. When the miners ran out, his was the only supply, and they paid the high price he asked. He did the same with the best quality Ames shovels arriving from the East. Another story described two discouraged miners who were selling out. They plodded into town and asked Huntington if he would buy their tent. He named a price and they agreed. He cleaned it and set it up with a FOR SALE sign on it. He cordially invited the men to sit in its shade while they waited for the stagecoach. Before they departed, they watched him sell the tent for five times what he had paid them.

Both Huntington and Hopkins were clean-living family men who had no yen whatsoever for the saloons and bawdyhouses of Sacramento. They regretted not having children of their own, and both eventually adopted. The Huntingtons raised Elizabeth's niece Clara from infancy, after her father died and her mother became very ill.

Huntington and Hopkins required that their salesclerks live cleanly, too. They were not reformers. They simply did not want bleary-eyed men nursing hangovers at the counter, nor men who had lost their wages gambling dipping into the cash register. After their twelve-hour shifts, the clerks lived in a dormitory

Mark Hopkins ran the hardware store while Huntington traveled in search of bargains.

in the back yard of the store. Elizabeth provided their meals. They signed a contract to stay off the streets at night. Huntington bought newspapers and books for them to read. The Huntingtons lived in an apartment above the store for many years.

Mark Hopkins was a vegetarian. It is not known whether he just didn't like meat, or if it was because he loved animals. He may have thought that meat was not good for him. It bothered him when he came to California that it was difficult to buy fresh vegetables. After settling in Sacramento, he bought some land on the river south of town and hired a gardener. The soil produced so much that Hopkins sold what he did not need. This land is a part of the vast Central Valley that today grows most of the fruits and vegetables consumed in the United States.

One day a black employee told Hopkins that his friend had been seized by a white man who said he was a runaway slave. The Fugitive Slave Law was being enforced then, and Hopkins, upset, quickly hired a lawyer for the man. He argued that the law was unconstitutional. The case went all the way to the California Supreme Court, but Hopkins lost.

After losing the case, Hopkins began to involve himself in local politics. He was elected a city alderman in 1856. That same year he joined Charles Crocker in forming the California Republican Party.

Huntington and Hopkins came to know Crocker and Stanford through their work with the Republican Party. Though Huntington was the only one of the four who never ran for public office, he also committed himself to the new Republican Party. He had hated slavery since witnessing it as a peddler in the South.

Chapter Three

Judah Goes "Crazy"

Two weeks after arriving in California, Ted Judah had completed his preliminary survey. The best route for the Sacramento Valley Railroad would be from Sacramento to Folsom. There would be a minimum of cuts, fills, and bridges, and the roadbed would only rise ten feet per mile as it moved northeast toward the foothills of the Sierras. A train cannot manage steep climbs. Judah wanted the trains to move rapidly, even when carrying heavy freight.

As the final surveying and estimating proceeded towards Folsom, Anna joined her husband. On weekends they rode into the foothills for exploration. While Judah scouted for passes for the transcontinental railroad, Anna sketched landscapes. She also collected flowers. Back in Sacramento, she pressed the flowers elegantly into scrapbooks and turned her sketches into oil paintings.

On February 12, 1855, work on the Sacramento Valley Railroad began. One day he came home with a ring with an inscription inside: *Sacramento Valley Railroad, March 4, 1855. First gold ever taken from earth in making a railroad bank.* On

June 15, after 130 days of sailing around South America, the first locomotive ever to be in California, the fifteen-ton *Sacramento,* arrived. A crowd shouted as it was hoisted from the ship and gently lowered to the ground.

Judah saw to it that excursion rides were soon available to the end of the track. He wanted to keep up the public's interest in the railroad. Unfortunately, there was a bank panic that put the Sacramento Valley Railroad stock in trouble. Though people flocked to ride the train, they were afraid of investing money. The railroad could not be continued beyond Folsom.

Judah knew it eventually would continue, despite the Wells-Fargo Company's efforts to keep the railroad out of their stage and freight line territories. Soon, the town of Folsom was booming, and the vast resources of lumber, coal, copper, marble, and granite in the mountains would need a railroad to haul them out.

Judah turned his eyes to the Sierras and said again to Anna, "Someday the railroad will run down one of these ridges. But which one? I am the man who will decide this."

Long before the coming of the railroad, people had sought a passage across the continent. The Lewis and Clark Expedition of 1804-5, that followed the Missouri River to the Continental Divide in the Northern Rockies and from there along the Snake and Columbia Rivers to the Oregon coast, greatly excited Americans. In 1845, the far-sighted Connecticut merchant Asa Whitney asked Congress for a land grant of 75 million acres to develop a railroad from Lake Michigan to Oregon. Congress

Theodore Judah searched years to find a pass through the Sierra Nevada Mountains.

voted no, partly because Southern states wanted the route to travel through their part of the country.

In 1853, Senators William Gwinn of California and Salmon Chase of Ohio got a specific sum of $150,000 for Army engineers to survey five possible railroad routes to the West. Though many scientists accompanied the surveys, *not a single railroad engineer went along!* The routes explored:

1. The northern route from St. Paul, Minnesota, to Seattle, Washington;

2. The central route from Council Bluffs, Iowa, to San Francisco, California;

3. The southern route from Fort Smith, Arkansas, to Los Angeles, California.

Theodore Judah was a Northerner. He thought it would be wrong to run the Pacific Railway through states where slavery existed. The railroad must bind free states and territories where all had equality of opportunity.

Judah thought the federal government should furnish the money for a real engineering survey of the central route. Once this was done, private business, not the government, should finance and build the railroad. He wrote down his arguments and gave them to Lauren Upson, the editor of the *Sacramento Union.* Upson printed Judah's articles and wrote many editorials himself about what was called Pacific Railroadism.

Judah continued to explore the Sierras with his surveying equipment. Sometimes he would be gone for several weeks.

In the fall of 1856, the Judahs stored their possessions and sailed to New York. This time they went through Panama, not

Nicaragua, on the new Aspinwall Railroad. Anna returned to Greenfield to see her family. Judah went to Washington, where he had a pamphlet printed, *A Practical Plan for Building the Pacific Railroad.* It argued for public money for the survey of one central route. Nobody listened, not even Senator Gwinn of California.

By the summer of 1857, the Judahs were back in California. Judah worked on extending the Sacramento Valley Railroad for Colonel Wilson. He talked wherever he could about the central route for the Pacific Railroad. People began to call him "that crazy engineer Judah" and then just "Crazy Judah."

He wanted a railway convention called by the California Legislature. His idea was to get Californians to agree on a central route in order to convince the U.S. Congress. Judah believed that this would break the deadlock between the slave states and the free states. He was elated when the Legislature finally voted on April 5, 1859, to hold a railway convention in San Francisco in September. He didn't mind the joke going around that the resolution passed just so the legislators could "get shed of that Crazy Judah." Anna *did* mind. She wanted her husband to have the respect he deserved.

While Anna painted one day, an idea came to her. Why not put on an exhibit advocating Judah's ideas. An artist knows that pictures can simplify complex ideas. She set to work preparing charts, maps, and graphs. For five months every surface of the apartment was covered with material. She took her husband's calculations and put them into easy-to-read tables. The viewer could compare, contrast, and understand.

She designed her portable "museum" for easy packing and assembling. When the railway convention opened in San Francisco on September 20, 1859, Anna stood by her exhibit. She answered questions, but mostly she listened. She heard what people with other interests thought. She knew they would have to be won over. She pointed out relevant figures in her charts. She mingled with the delegates and their wives. She kept a careful poll in her head.

After ten days, she reported to her husband that she felt sure the official convention delegates would vote to support his central route. This was the time to call for the vote. She was right. The vote taken on October 11, 1859, supported Judah's idea, and also appointed him to be the representative to take the recommendation to Congress.

The Judahs sailed for Washington on the *Sonora*. The new California Congressman John Burch happened to be on board along with Senator Lane of Oregon. Judah easily won over Congressman Burch to the central route, but Senator Lane was another matter. Oregonians naturally favored the northern route. However, one evening at dinner, Senator Lane admitted that it might be a good idea to start the central route first.

Anna's heart jumped when she heard this. Her charts and paintings, and Ted's fossil, mineral and ore collections, flashed into her mind. She had packed all in their luggage. Might there be any advantage in establishing a Pacific Railway Museum on Capitol Hill? Others might come to the same conclusion.

By November, the Pacific Railway Museum was set up in the Capitol. Judah was there to answer questions. Hundreds

Anna Judah set up the Pacific Railway Museum on Capitol Hill in Washington D.C.

visited, but Congress was distracted. The country was simmering with divisiveness; the Civil War was on the horizon. "Forget the railroad, young man," President Buchanan told Judah, "until we see what is going to happen to the nation."

In February, Judah's spirit was revived by a message from a second railroad convention in Sacramento. He was instructed to help the California Congressmen introduce a bill Judah had originally written. It proposed the following:

1. Government guarantee of 5% interest for people who invested their money in the Pacific Railway;

2. Railroad to be completed in 10 years;

3. Land grants to the railroad to encourage settlers and raise more money;

4. Carrying the U.S. mail at low rates.

By April the bill was introduced but was immediately tabled until the next session. Congress felt it had too many other problems. Judah was discouraged. But on April 14, 1860, came the news of the Pony Express. In ten days riders had crossed the central route to California.

Judah saw this as proof of feasibility for a railroad. While waiting for the next Congress and a new President, he felt he must find the specific pass through the Sierras, and make cost estimates which they could not refuse. He decided to return to California.

Finding the right pass through the mountains led Judah down may false trails. The range of the Sierras that had to be crossed consisted of two granite walls with a trough between. In some places the trough was fifty miles wide. Judah had been searching for a pass that cut through both granite walls. Niagara's Gorge was child's play compared to this challenge.

After returning from one discouraging trip, Anna handed Judah a letter from Dr. Daniel Strong, a pharmacist who lived in the mining village of Dutch Flat. Dr. Strong had a found a spine ridge rising between two river valleys on the western side. The rivers were the Yuba (south fork) and the American (north fork). This ridge was a long, gradual incline that went from the Sacramento plain to a 6,690 foot summit.

Judah and Dr. Strong traveled to the pass. When the two men reached the top of the ridge, called the "Emigrant Trail", they gazed down at an enchanted sight—a sun bedazzled sapphire lake set in a green ring of great fir trees. Beyond, the snow-covered peaks rose 2000 feet. To the southeast they could see

Dutch Flat was the home of Judah's friend Dr. Strong.

the Truckee River, which flowed north from Lake Tahoe.

The magnitude of the discovery hit Judah, standing there under the brilliant cloud-splashed blue sky in the fragrant wind of the mighty Sierra Nevada. It was a moment he would never forget. The Snowy Range was like a halo around him. He took a deep breath in the thin altitude and thought about his conclusion: This ridge, with engineered modifications, would bring the Pacific Railroad up the western wall. This lake shore would lead it gently through the trough. The Truckee River valley would take it down to the Nevada desert.

Dr. Strong pointed toward the body of water. "That's Donner Lake. This is where the Donner Party perished in the awful winter of '46."

The two men continued to survey. Judah wanted as much data as he could get on every foot of the pass. Dr. Strong was an excellent assistant. They mapped elevations and the sites of tunnels and cuts, took rock samples and labeled them carefully. Days passed.

One night, Dr. Strong was awakened by stillness. He had spent so much time in the mountains that his ears were attuned to the forest noises while he slept. Suddenly there were none. Heavy snowflakes blotted out all sound.

In a swirling whiteness more terrifying than night, the men let their horses lead them to safety. Judah let his mind dwell on his railroad. At dawn, safe in the little town of Dutch Flat, he heard Dr.Strong telling people that they had barely escaped the snowstorm alive.

Inside Strong's Drugstore, Judah spread and sorted his notes. He mumbled, estimated, and scribbled. Customers came and went. Dr. Strong chatted and prescribed remedies. Finally, Judah laid down his pen and looked up. His intuition had been correct. The railroad would cross the Sierra Nevada mountains through the Donner Pass.

Chapter Four

The Central Pacific—Born At Last!

Judah finished his pamphlet, written to persuade investors to take a chance on the Central Pacific Railroad, a few days before Abraham Lincoln was elected as the first Republican president. California law stated that before a railroad could be legally formed as a corporation, $1000 in investment stock must be raised for each mile of the proposed line. It was 116 miles from Sacramento to the Nevada border. $116,000 was a great deal of money in 1860.

The people of tiny Dutch Flat had responded to the stock sale enthusiastically. They respected Dr. Strong, and when he put his money into the new railroad, so did they—for a total of $46,500. Judah thought he would have no trouble raising the remaining $70,000 from the bankers and ship owners of San Francisco.

Judah was wrong. Business leaders thought the investment too risky. Seven years to build a railroad across the granite Sierras? Impossible. Twenty years was more like it. They wanted to earn more money *now*.

Judah was angry, but not about to give up. He returned to

Sacramento, where he knew that the most successful business-men were increasing the political power of the new Republican Party. He knew they were former New Yorkers like himself. They did not want California to join the new Confederacy.

Collis Huntington was intrigued by Judah's plans and de-cided to approach Crocker, Hopkins, and Stanford. "I'll see which way the cat will jump," replied Charlie Crocker after listening to Judah's proposal. Ever cautious, Mark Hopkins stroked his wispy beard and said, "That mountain offers a vast amount of work." Leland Stanford felt more comfortable about a gigantic enterprise when like-minded men were with him on the risk. To Judah's joy, these men, whom history would later call the Big Four, decided to invest.

On April 30, 1861, the first organizational meeting of the Central Pacific stockholders met at the Huntington and Hopkins Hardware Store. They elected Leland Stanford, President, Collis Huntington, Vice-President, Mark Hopkins, Treasurer, and Theodore Judah, Chief Engineer. On June 27, 1861, the State of California granted The Central Pacific Railroad corpo-ration status. A railroad now existed on paper.

Collis Huntington was the smartest, and the toughest, of the Big Four. He knew he was the best qualified for president of the railroad, and he was surprised that the nominating commit-tee of Judah and Strong named Stanford. Huntington did not like Judah, a man so different from himself in education and temperament, and realized that Judah wanted a more agreeable man in the top spot.

All summer of 1861, Ted Judah was out surveying with his

Charlie Crocker's construction company built most of the Central Pacific.

crew. Anna was often with him, riding muleback and sketching. Her paintings of Donner Lake were used as the illustrations on the first Central Pacific stock certificates.

The railroad required a tremendous amount of re-checking and coordinating. Judah was never sloppy. Mistakes could turn into costly repairs. On October 9, 1861, he reported his cost estimate to the board—$41 million. Even for wealthy men, this was an enormous sum. They voted to send Judah to Washington to see that the Railroad Act was passed so they could count on government help.

When Judah told Anna about the upcoming trip to Washington, she was not surprised. She had expected it. Both she and Judah were pleased that Congressman Aaron Sargent would be sailing with them. He could turn out to be very helpful.

The Judahs soon won Sargent over to the Central Pacific's cause. Everything was smooth sailing, except for detour east of Cuba and Bermuda made necessary by the Confederate ironclads patrolling the South Atlantic coast. The first shot of the Civil War had been fired when the Confederates took Fort Sumter at Charleston, South Carolina, on April 12, 1861.

The Judahs sat together in the reopened Railway Museum in the Capitol. She had brought new paintings and plants from the Sierras. Judah had updated surveys and costs. People streamed through. Anna was a knowledgeable guide.

Meanwhile, the Confederates were winning battles. Arkansas and Texas joined the Confederacy. The Pony Express became obsolete when the transcontinental telegraph was completed in Salt Lake City in October, 1861. News of Leland

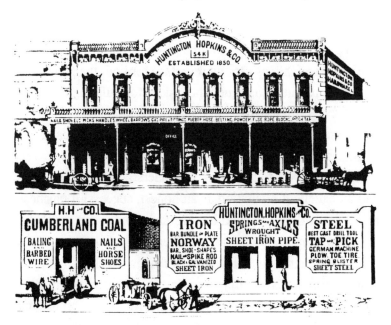

Huntington, Hopkins & Co. was located at 54 K Street in Sacremento.

Stanford's election as Republican governor of California came to Washington over the wires.

Northern Congressmen got a morale boost and assurance that the West would stay with the Union. They passed three very important laws to satisfy these needs:

1. The Morrill Act, which gave states land and money for colleges of agriculture;

2. The Homestead Act, which gave 160 acres of Western land to any citizen who claimed it, erected a house, cultivated the land, and resided on it for five years;

3. The Pacific Railroad Act.

The time had finally arrived, and Ted Judah was there as "accredited agent" of the Central Pacific. No one knew more than he about railroad building and writing railroad laws. He worked feverishly as official secretary for both the House and Senate Committees assigned the task of formulating the wording of the Railroad Act.

When it was clear that the bill would be voted on, Judah wired Huntington, who came to Washington. Huntington was very persuasive in one-to-one talks. He understood finances, and he had an excellent reputation as an honest, successful businessman who had always paid his Eastern suppliers.

There were no longer any Southerners in Congress to vote against the Sierra route. It was clear that an overland link to the resources of California was in the country's interest. However, Thaddeus Stevens, the powerful House representative from Pennsylvania, a state that manufactured iron, insisted on adding an amendment to the bill that required all materials used in railroad construction to be American made.

This amendment turned out to be a terrible setback for the railroad. The Union Army had priority for all such supplies, including the blasting powder needed to make tunnels through the granite mountains. Huntington, who was in charge of purchasing material for the Central Pacific, had to nag constantly, and to pay highly inflated prices, to get the supplies he needed. Had he been able to buy them in England, where the rails were available, less expensive, and of superior quality, the great iron link would have been built much more quickly and for less money.

The Pacific Railroad Act granted land to the railroad, guaranteed loans, determined that the Union Pacific Company

An early Central Pacific check signed by Judah and Hopkins.

would build west from the Missouri River to meet the east-bound Central Pacific at the California-Nevada border. It also committed the railroads to priority transportation of U.S. mails, Army troops and supplies.

On June 20, 1862, the Pacific Railroad Act passed in the Senate, and on June 24 in the House of Representatives. Judah wired to Governor Stanford: WE HAVE DRAWN THE ELEPHANT. NOW LET US SEE IF WE CAN HARNESS IT UP.

After the Pacific Railroad Act was signed into law by President Lincoln on July 2, Huntington and Judah went to New York City to "shop" for the new railroad. Huntington learned from Judah about locomotives. Judah already knew that Huntington would never buy a thing that was not needed. He smiled as Huntington grumbled about "the confounded fooforaws" of gilt lettering and painted scenes.

Judah had not smiled a year earlier when he showed the four men the blueprints for an office and museum in Sacramento. Judah had budgeted $12,000 for the building. He thought it was important to maintain public interest in the railroad. Stanford liked the plans and agreed that public image was important. But Huntington had angrily sketched a design for a simple shed and stalked out of the meeting. The shed, and not the office Judah had wanted, was built.

Chapter Five

The "Elephant" Begins to Creep

The ground-breaking ceremonies for the Central Pacific Railroad took place on a rainy January 8, 1863. Charlie Crocker was the master of ceremonies. After listening to six long speeches, Crocker decided to liven things up before letting the crowd leave. He ordered "nine hearty cheers," then concluded: "This is no idle ceremony; the pile driver is now driving piles for the foundation of the bridge across the American River.... All of my own strength, intellect, and energy is devoted to the building of this railroad."

Crocker meant what he said. He admitted he knew nothing about engineering: "I could not have measured a cut any more than I could have flown!" But he could provide the chief engineer with men and materials. He was a good boss. So he founded the Crocker Construction Company and plunged in.

Crocker soon seemed to be everywhere. Each day he rode the work line on his big sorrel horse. "I used to go up and down...like a mad bull, stopping along the way wherever there was anything amiss and raising Old Nick with the boys who were not up to the time," he wrote later. "If it becomes necessary to jump off a dock in service of the company, instead of saying *Go, boys*, you must pull off your coat and say *Come, boys,* and let them follow you."

Though the workers liked Crocker, Theodore Judah was often not happy with the quality of work performed by Crocker Construction Company.

Judah had trusted his partners enough to seal their agreements with a handshake. But he soon began developing doubts about the Big Four after he agreed to start a wagon road through Donner Pass that would carry railroad supplies and earn tolls from other traffic as well. Judah hoped to assure these "shopkeepers" of some profits early on. By 1863, Judah heard rumors that the Big Four were satisfied with the wagon road—so satisfied they were questioning the wisdom of building the railroad. Newspapers printed the rumors. There was a panic; many people sold their Central Pacific stock. Dr. Strong sold his stock and resigned from the Board of Directors. Although the "shopkeepers" continued with the railroad, this disturbance upset Judah.

Judah also disagreed with a method Huntington had to collect more money. The Railroad Act said the government would provide additional money for each mile of the rail line built from where the base of the Sierras began because of the greater difficulty, and expense, in cutting through the mountains. Judah judged this point to be where the first granite outcropping appeared, twenty-two miles east of Sacramento. Governor Stanford went to the State Geologist, who said that the base began where the brown dirt of the Sacramento Valley met the

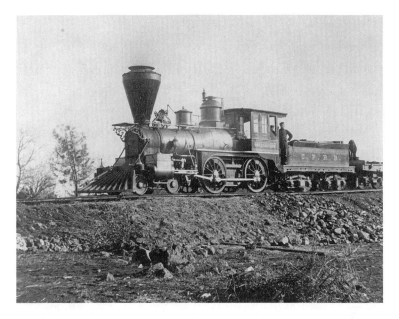

The locomotive *Governor Stanford* was one of the first purchased by the Central Pacific.

red soil of the Sierras, only seven miles east of Sacramento. The Department of the Interior agreed with the geologist, and the Central Pacific got more money, which it badly needed. Judah, however, felt the truth had been twisted.

Judah also worried about the "holding company" set up by the Big Four. Central Pacific stocks were selling slowly. Huntington decided that the only way to get credit was to incorporate a holding company called The Associates. This meant that the Big Four would handle all Central Pacific contracts. For example, The Associates decided that Crocker's new construction company would get the contract for grading and laying track. The pay for this would make Crocker's company successful. Other businessmen who were reluctant to do business with the railroad because its stock was not selling would be willing to extend credit to Crocker because of his reputation for business success. Eventually, the Big Four bought out the other Central Pacific shareholders.

Another clash between Judah and Huntington occurred in May 1863. Huntington returned from a New York trip to find that Judah had changed the rail line in Sacramento to run directly to the river docks. This was more sensible but also more expensive. Judah thought it was penny wise and pound foolish to re-route later, but Huntington disagreed. He hurried to the construction site and stalked up to Judah: "It will cost $200,000 to put the road here. We cannot afford that at this time!" He turned to the foreman. "Shift your men. The road will go up I Street as originally planned."

Judah was furious. He snapped, "You are but one member of the board of directors. I am the chief engineer!"

Huntington tightened his lips. "There will be no work done on this road until it goes up I Street."

It went up I Street.

The final blow to Judah's trust of the Big Four came when Hopkins told Judah that he had not paid the required amount to purchase the stock he owned. Judah reminded him angrily that they had agreed that Judah would not have to pay cash for his shares because of his long hours spent surveying and promoting to get the Central Pacific started.

Mark Hopkins answered that he kept the company records and there was nothing in writing about Judah's arrangement.

Judah exploded. He shouted at the Big Four and they at him.

Huntington told him that either he should buy them out or they would buy him out. Each man's share was valued at $100,000. They would give him the first chance to raise $400,000. Judah agreed. He felt these men were betraying "his" railroad. Since 1855 he had been explorer, surveyor, engineer, law-writer, secretary, and lobbyist. Anna had been collector, record keeper, and museum maker. Now these men wanted him to be only the Chief Engineer.

Anna agreed that it was worth a trip back East to raise the money and to regain control. Judah left his engineering duties in the hands of Samuel S. Montague, a New Englander who had worked his way west.

On October 2, 1863 Theodore and Anna sailed for New York on the steamer *St. Louis*. Near Acapulco, Mexico, the *St. Louis* met a northbound schooner *Herald of the Morning*. Judah watched it from the railing, but he did not know that it carried the first 100 tons of rails for the Central Pacific Railroad.

The sky was full of thunderclouds as the Judahs rode the Aspinwall Railroad across Panama. At the Caribbean pier where their ship awaited them, the rain came in a deluge. The torrent went on and on. Ted grew impatient, bought a giant black umbrella, and escorted the women and children onto the ship.

When everyone was aboard and the ship moving, Ted complained of a headache and went to bed.

Anna searched for the ship's doctor. Terror sent her head spinning when the doctor examined him and said that Ted had contracted Yellow Fever. There was nothing to do but keep him comfortable and hope for the best.

Anna sat by him for eight days, bathing him with cool water, changing his bedclothes.

On October 26, as the first Central Pacific rails were being laid by Crocker's men, the ship docked in New York City. Anna allowed her spirits to rise. They had hotel reservations, and she knew a doctor, an old family friend. She sent for him immediately, and the ship's doctor helped her get Judah to the Metropolitan Hotel.

Dr. F. N. Otis arrived. But it was too late. On the morning of November 2, 1863, Judah died. He was 37 years old.

Ted's death was the front page news of the *Sacramento Union*. The Big Four passed a resolution of sympathy to Anna and appointed Samuel Montague new Chief Engineer.

A grieving Anna took his body back up the Connecticut River Valley to Greenfield on the railroad her husband had built.

"He rests from his labors" she had inscribed on his tomb in the Pierce Family plot in the Federal Street Cemetery. Vigorous, hard-driving Judah might have chosen "We kept the ball rolling," but a grieving Anna wanted dignity.

Chapter Six

Across the Sierras

By 1864 a serious labor shortage had developed. Most of the men available for construction work preferred to try their luck in the mines. Silver had been discovered in Nevada, and many men signed up for the railroad just to get a ride to the camp at the end of the tracks. During the summer of 1864, 1,900 out of the 2,000 men hired vanished over the mountains. The Civil War also kept great numbers of men in the Union and Confederate armies. Crocker even petitioned the U.S. War Department for 5,000 prisoners of war to come west and work, but was turned down. He finally was able to recruit some Irish immigrants to sail on to California. But the shortage of workers was a continual problem.

Leland Stanford wanted to hire Chinese men. There were nearly 50,000 Chinese men in California. Most of them worked as servants, cooks, and small farmers. Some ran laundries; others were fishermen, merchants, cigar makers, and miners. Many Californians referred to the Chinese as "Celestials," after the name "Celestial Kingdom" that some Chinese had given to their homeland.

Crocker liked the idea of hiring Chinese. The Celestials had a reputation for thrift, hard work, and honesty. But Superintendent James Strobridge scoffed. He pointed out that the Chinese were small. How could they possibly do such hard work?

Charlie Crocker's answer was: "They built the Great Wall of China, didn't they? That was almost as tough a job as this railroad, wasn't it?"

Strobridge insisted on a test. A gang of fifty Chinese men worked on a section while a gang of Irish men worked on another. At the end of the month, the Chinese had done smoother grading and more of it. Strobridge admitted he had been wrong.

Most of the Chinese immigrants had left China because of bloody civil wars and feuds. Their trip to America was usually difficult and expensive. An agent in China would lend the money for the trip. After arriving in California, the immigrant signed up with one of the so-called Chinese Six Companies. The company helped with banking, medical needs, and legal aid; it also supplied Chinese foods. When the debt, plus interest, had been paid back, usually after a period of four to five years, the immigrant was free to return to China or to stay in the United States.

After hiring the Chinese to work on the Central Pacific, Crocker hired Sam Thayer, who spoke several Chinese dialects. He interpreted between the Chinese and their American bosses. He also taught English to the Chinese crew leaders.

Crocker agreed to pay the Chinese $26 per month. Later, when they went on strike and demanded $40, Crocker flew into a rage and withheld their food. Despite his dramatics, he eventually offered $35 per month, which they accepted.

Crocker also saw to it that the workers got their Chinese foods from San Francisco, and he was good to his word that he would return the body of any man who died to the Chinese cemeteries in San Francisco. The men believed that if their bones were not returned home, their spirits could never be at rest.

The Chinese stayed remarkably healthy. Each gang of twenty had its own cook. The water they drank was first boiled and made into tea. The workers could have it any time they wished from tea-boys who roamed the construction site with tea kegs slung from a yoke. At the end of the work day, each man went to an old whiskey barrel the cook had prepared for him with hot water. He bathed and received fresh clothes. Their menu included dried oysters, cuttlefish, bamboo sprouts, rice, crackers, salted cabbage, vermicelli, poultry and dried fruit. After supper, they would play fan-tan and lottery games until bedtime.

Generally, the Chinese did the grading, cuts and fills, blasting of rocks, and tree-chopping. The Americans and the Irish kept the better-paying skilled jobs like carpentry (bridge and trestle building), masonry (culverts and tunnel entrances) and track laying. The Chinese worked with steady rhythm. They soon became the largest work-force ever assembled in America.

The Central Pacific would never have been completed without the Chinese workers. The task sometimes seemed impossible. The Sierra Nevada, which means "Snowy Range" in Spanish, might equally well be called the Granite Range. The hard rock created a tremendous challenge to men working with

The Chinese were the largest work-force ever assembled in America.

Chinese workers had to break through granite to reach Summit Tunnel.

Superintendent James Strobridge resisted employing Chinese workers.

picks, axes, ropes, wheelbarrows, carts, mules, and explosives.

The first great obstacle was Cape Horn, a gigantic cliff that reared 1000 feet straight up from the American River, blocking the railroad's path as it wound its way through the mountains. It had to be moved out of the way. Men were lowered from the top in little chairs to drill holes and tamp in blasting powder. After lighting the long fuses, they would yell to be pulled up quickly. Sometimes the fuses burned too fast, and a worker would be blown up.

One day in the summer of 1865, a Chinese crew leader asked Strobridge if his workers could have a try working with the explosives. Chinese laborers had built cliff fortresses for centuries in the Yangtze River gorges; their techniques had been passed down. They were used to working with gunpowder, a Chinese invention.

Strobridge agreed, and ordered the reeds the men used to weave their own baskets, with four strong eyelets at the top for the hauling ropes to go through. They became a common sight moving up and down the face of the cliff. Their drills rat-tatted in the clear mountain air, followed by the *crump!* of explosions that sent granite shards flying into the valley. Before winter set in, the Chinese had conquered Cape Horn. In the spring, the track layers swarmed in ahead of schedule, and trains moved toward the 7000 ft. summit at Donner Lake.

Fifteen tunnels had to be made at the summit; the longest was 1,659 feet. For nearly two years, four crews worked from both ends of the tunnel and from a hole bored at the center. They worked round the clock, summer and winter. Inside the earth the weather never changed, and it was always night. It was grueling, dusty, and punishing to the lungs.

They decided to try a new liquid explosive called nitroglycerine. It was far more effective than blasting powder, but it was dangerous to handle. Many men were killed. When Strobridge lost an eye in an explosion, Crocker ordered them to return to using powder. The progress averaged eight inches a day. Finally, on May 3, 1867, the last stubborn remnant of the east facing crumbled away. The summit had been pierced. The Chinese workers let out wave after wave of cheers.

The mountain winters presented a different challenge. The winter of '64-'65 was mild, but blizzards the next two winters dumped fifteen feet of snow. Drifts rose to sixty feet. The tunnel

An inside view of one of the snow tunnels built for winter work in the Sierra Nevada Mountains.

Wagons were responsible for hauling supplies to the workers at Summit Tunnel.

workers lived in snow tunnels, with stove pipes and air holes poking through. Avalanches could sweep away a camp in seconds. Bodies were found in the spring thaw with work tools still clutched in frozen hands.

When outside work could be resumed, a new task was the building of thirty-eight miles of snow sheds over the tracks. These were made of redwood. Some were still in use in the 1950s. While battling the elements, Crocker still kept his eye open to opportunities. All this snow and ice? He created the Summit Ice Company. Packed in sawdust, the big blocks were shipped to California cities. Oddly, this business did not make profits, because ice from Alaska sent by boat cost less. But Crocker's efforts to build reservoirs and irrigation channels from Sierra snow melt were successful and opened many acres

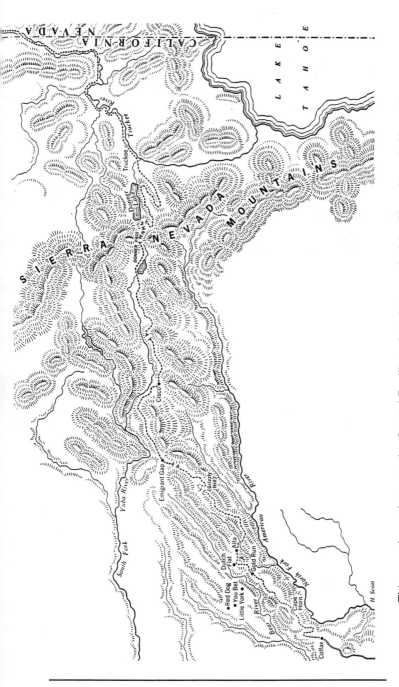

This map shows the route the Central Pacific took to the summit of the Sierra Nevada Mountains.

of dry land for farms and vineyards.

It is remarkable that four men as strong-willed as the Big Four could have stayed united throughout the project. One reason for their success was the division of labor. Crocker virtually lived at the construction site as overseer. Huntington was positioned on the East Coast to push for the Railroad Acts of 1862 and 1864, and to buy the needed rails and equipment. Stanford was involved in California politics, and tried to keep public opinion favorable to the railroad. Hopkins was book-keeper and financial advisor.

Only occasionally did one of the Big Four interfere in another's area. One such time involved a compressed steam drill. Construction on the Union Pacific started in 1865, nearly two years after the Central Pacific. The Union Pacific's terrain for the first 500 miles was the Great Plains, land so flat that it looked as if it was designed for a railroad. The Central Pacific had to deal with the granite, the cliffs, and the snow of the Sierras. The Union Pacific made more rapid progress.

It made the Big Four nervous to hear of the Union Pacific's progress. Stanford became excited one day in 1866 when an inventor demonstrated his new steam drilling machine in San Francisco. Stanford thought the new invention could speed their progress. He sent the man and drill to Summit Tunnel, where blasting and hand drills were clearing a measly eight inches a day.

James Strobridge disagreed with Stanford about the new machine. He refused to disrupt his operation to try it. Crocker backed Strobridge, and angry letters were exchanged between

Trains were equipped with snow plows to clear the tracks.

the men. When Strobridge said that connecting the drill would stop the hoist engine that removed loose rock from the center bore, Stanford bought another hoisting engine and sent it up the mountains. Strobridge still would not change his mind. Stanford probably ground his teeth in frustration when he heard reports and saw pictures of the Union Pacific's successful use of steam shovels.

Chapter Seven

On To Promontory

While the Central Pacific was toiling in the Sierras, the Union Pacific moved west across the Great Plains from Omaha, Nebraska. What one company had, the other did not. The Union Pacific had flat land for the most part, but it did not have wood for ties and trestles, or good stone for culverts and track fill. It also had to deal with hostile Sioux and Cheyenne tribes, who were furious about the loss of their lands.

For labor, the Union Pacific hired Irish immigrants who were fleeing famine and British rule in their country. There were also ex-Confederate and Union soldiers, Mexicans, and African Americans. Eventually, they would all come to be called "gandy dancers" for their rhythmic movements laying rail with tools made by the Gandy Company of Chicago.

The Railroad Acts of 1862 and 1864 gave the railroads a certain amount of money and land per mile of track laid, so naturally both companies wanted to cover the most land. The Big Four were especially eager to get "easy" money for the flat miles in the Nevada and Utah desert that would be child's play after the mountain hazards.

Before Summit Tunnel was finished, Crocker had workers go to the eastern side to start preparing the road bed through Donner Pass and along the Truckee River that wound gently downward into the Nevada desert. He had locomotives, cars and supplies hauled by sleds and wagons to the new tracks. When Summit Tunnel was completed, the tracks were connected, and the Central Pacific was able to collect large amounts of government money.

In October, 1868, Vice-President Thomas Durant of the Union Pacific was proud of his workers' achievement in laying almost eight miles of track in one day. He cabled a bet to Crocker, whose men were then laying about four miles a day. Durant wagered $10,000 that the Union Pacific record could not be broken. Crocker thought a few minutes, chuckled, and wired back an acceptance. The bet was on, as long as he could choose the place and day. Though the Central Pacific's best single day record was six miles, Crocker stated they would lay ten.

Crocker waited until they were only fourteen miles away from Promontory, Utah, where the Central Pacific was to meet the Union Pacific. He had Strobridge carefully arrange supplies and prepare his men. On April 28, 1869, the epic event began at dawn.

The road bed had already been prepared. In perfect rhythm, ties were taken from wagons and placed on the bed. Rails followed, to be spiked in and reinforced with "fishplates." Every man had one thing to do in an exact order. Relief men stood waiting to fill in for any who could not keep pace. Small rocks called ballast were added and tamped as the "ironmen" moved

Central Pacific workers laying tracks and telegraph poles during the race toward Promontory Point.

ahead. When the sun set at 7 p.m., the whistle blew. "Lay off!" Strobridge yelled.

Exactly 10 miles and 200 feet of rails had been laid. The Central Pacific's Irish and Chinese workers had placed 25,800 ties, driven 55,000 spikes, and screwed on 7,040 fishplates. The eight Irish "ironmen," who did not use a single relief man, had lifted 2 million pounds of rail! Crocker had won his bet. His men had set a record that has never been surpassed, even with today's machines.

The merging of the railroads was to occur on May 8, 1869. But on May 6th, Union Pacific workers, angry over not being paid, halted Vice-President Thomas Durant's train en-route to Promontory. They removed him from his car and held him hostage until their wages were paid. The arrangements required two days. Durant was released unharmed, but severe rains on May 8th made the roadbeds and bridges unsafe. The ceremony had to be delayed.

Meanwhile, on May 6th, Leland Stanford's special train with dignitaries made its way to Promontory, chugging a few miles behind the regularly scheduled Central Pacific passenger train. East of Truckee, workers clearing trees beside the tracks saw the first train go by and assumed the tracks would be free for rolling logs downhill. A fifty-footer fell onto the track. Before the workers could get the log off, Stanford's train came around the curve. The engineer was able to brake, but the engine was damaged. Stanford's car was carried on to Promontory by another engine, but the guests, one of whom was seriously injured, were shaken. Because of the Union Pacific's troubles,

The last rail is laid at Promontory Point, Utah.

however, they had plenty of time to recover.

Between 10 and 11 a.m. on May 10, 1869, two Union Pacific trains arrived at Promonotory, Utah with soldiers bound for the San Francisco Presidio and a band in bright new uniforms. The Central Pacific *Jupiter* arrived at 11:15 a.m., bearing the last spikes and tie. Almost fifteen hundred people assembled at the spot, while the *Jupiter* and Union Pacific No. 119 pulled up. The sun had heated the sagebrush flat to a pleasant 69 degrees.

Across the United States, telegraph lines were kept open for the news. People awaited the moment. The telegraph operator kept them informed. About noon he tapped :

> TO EVERYBODY. KEEP QUIET. WHEN THE LAST SPIKE IS DRIVEN AT PROM-ONTORY POINT WE WILL SAY 'DONE!' DON'T BREAK THE CIRCUIT. BUT WATCH FOR THE SIGNALS OF THE BLOWS OF THE HAMMER.

A wire had been placed on the tie, so that when the Golden Spike was struck, the blow would trigger a magnetic ball to fall from the dome of the Capitol in Washington D.C.

> ALMOST READY. HATS OFF. PRAYER IS BEING OFFERED.

The prayers and speeches went on and on. At 12:40 the operator was finally able to say:

> WE HAVE GOT DONE PRAYING. THE SPIKE IS ABOUT TO BE PRESENTED.

The final tie was made of silver plated laurel wood. A commenorative spike of silver from Nevada's Comstock Lode was first tapped: "To the iron of the East and the gold of the West, Nevada adds her link of silver to span the continent and weld the oceans," said the governor of Nevada. Then from Arizona came an alloy spike of gold, silver, and iron.

At 12:47 Leland Stanford nervously struck down with the silver hammer at the golden spike—and missed! He hit the rail with a clang. But the telegraph operator had had enough waiting. He closed the circuit himself, notifying "Done!" across the land. Stanford's second blow hit, and the spike went in. The ball fell from the Capitol dome and the cracked Liberty Bell rang in Philadelphia's Independence Hall. Guns and cannons boomed. Bells tolled. Fireworks exploded. Everywhere people whooped, cheered, danced, and sang "The Star-Spangled Banner."

Photos were taken of the two locomotives cowcatcher-to-cowcatcher. Two days later, in his San Francisco newspaper office, Bret Harte looked at the now-famous Golden Spike picture and wondered:

> What was it the engines said,
> Pilots touching, head to head,
> Facing on a single track,
> Half a world behind each back?

Charlie Crocker chose to remain in Sacramento and to not attend the celebration in Utah. Over the past six years he had never spent more than three nights in a row in his own bed. He had become an insomniac while his mind raced, trying to figure ways to speed up the job. "I went to bed and slept like a child,"

The famous photograph captured the engineers of the Central

Pacific and the Union Pacific shaking hands on Golden Spike Day.

he reported. Nor did he forget the Chinese workers.

> I wish to call to mind that the early completion
> of this railroad we have built has been in a great
> measure due to . . . the Chinese—to the fidelity
> and industry they have shown—and the great
> amount of laborers of this land that have been
> employed upon the work.

Anna Judah was at her husband's grave in Greenfield, Massachusetts when the Golden Spike was driven. May 10, 1869, was also their 22nd wedding anniversary. This remarkable coincidence was very special to Anna.

Later the California historian H. H. Bancroft described the situation before the transcontinental railroad:

The sunburnt immigrant, walking with his wife and little ones beside his gaunt
and weary oxen in mid-continent, the sea-sick traveler, the homesick bride
whose wedding trip had included a passage of the Isthmus, the merchant whose
stock needed replenishing; everyone prayed for a Pacific Railroad!

The prayers on May 10, 1869, were those of jubilation and thanksgiving. An American could now go from sea to sea in eight days.

Chapter Eight

All The Traffic Will Bear

Even before the Golden Spike was driven, the Big Four had begun thinking about how to guarantee that the Central Pacific would turn a profit. There were three major problems.

1. They had been counting on the Far East trade that would come across the Pacific and transfer to train for the overland trip to the Atlantic coast. But the Suez Canal, which connected the Red Sea to the Mediterranean and provided easier sea access, opened the same month the railroad was completed—May 1869.

2. The Nevada silver mines were producing less.

3. Payments on bonds had to be met.

The first battle had been to get the railroad built. Now the struggle was to make certain it survived. The best way to guarantee survival was to eliminate any competitors.

This system of eliminating competitors is called a monopoly, and the Big Four were able to create one for several years. They bought the small railroads that already existed in California—the Sacramento Valley, the California Central, the Western Pacific, and the San Francisco & San Jose. They built the

California & Oregon Railroad up the Sacramento Valley north to Portland, and the San Joaquin Railroad south through land that became richly productive as farmers built irrigation systems. These two roads were the beginning of the Southern Pacific Railroad that was built east from Los Angeles to New Orleans.

The Big Four also had "a fence around the harbor" at Oakland for thirty years, which meant that ships unloading had to use their facilities. Then they started a shipping line across the Pacific Ocean.

Once the railroad had a monopoly in place, it could charge whatever they wanted to those who needed to move goods on their railroads. Farmers and businessmen had no other way to get their products to market. When those paying the higher rates protested to political leaders, their complaints fell on deaf ears because the Big Four financially supported politicians who favored their railroads. Huntington insisted there was nothing wrong in contributing money or railroad passes to politicians whose ideas were like his own. He felt this was quite different from bribery, the buying of a specific vote or favor with money.

By the early 1870's, the Big Four's railroads had established a principle called "all the traffic will bear" that they used to set their freight rates. For example, if farmers had a good harvest, the rates would be high; after a bad harvest, rates would be low. Railroad agents kept careful watch on farmers, miners, and businessmen, setting rates so that the customers could stay in business and make a little profit, but not very much. This infuriated the hard-working people who wanted to get ahead in

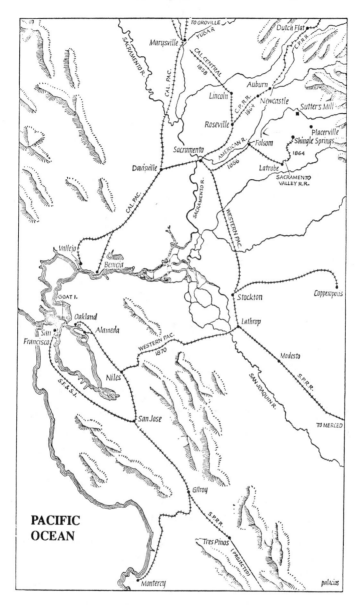

After completing the Central Pacific the Big Four took control of competing California railroads.

a country that supposedly had a free-enterprise economic system.

Here are two examples of how the Big Four operated their railroad. A load of pig iron shipped from Hankow, China, cost only four dollars per ton to go across the Pacific Ocean to the port of San Pedro near Los Angeles. The railroad charged two dollars per ton to take the load on a forty-five minute trip to Los Angeles. Miners asked for the cost of shipping quartz 300 miles to San Francisco. They were told fifty dollars per car. When they shipped more than three car loads, the rate was raised to $73 per car. They paid and shipped more carloads. Then the price jumped to $100. The miners went to the agent and said this rate would shut them down. The agent asked to see their books so he could set a rate that would keep them in business and allow the railroad to make its maximum profit.

The novelist Frank Norris wrote *The Octopus* to depict the struggle the wheat farmers in the San Joaquin Valley had with the railroad. Norris took the title from one of the favorite images the railroad's critics used to depict it. Hogs, monsters, and camels were other images used by the San Francisco *Examiner*, which became famous for its attacks on the Big Four, especially Huntington and Stanford.

Over the years, people did what they could to break the Railroad's control. The people of San Francisco never let them gain control of their harbor as they had in Oakland. In 1885, sheep ranchers organized and sent their wool 300 miles on wagons to San Francisco.

In March of 1887, Congress established the Pacific Railway

An example of a typical anti-Big Four cartoon published in the San Francisco *Examiner.*

Commission to regulate the railroad. The Commission was given the power to hire expert help, to summon witnesses and records, and to require changes. Crocker, Huntington, and Stanford argued vigorously that they had done nothing illegal. Stanford even claimed that the government owed them $62 million. He said that the Central Pacific had been completed seven years early, and they had not claimed the money they would have received had they delayed. The Commission criticized the railroad's business practices.

The Interstate Commerce Commission was created in 1887 to regulate all carriers that hauled goods between states. In 1906, the Hepburn Act gave the Commission the power to set rates.

In 1893, a "People's Railroad" was started to break the monopoly. The 300-mile Valley Railroad started in the San Joaquin Valley and traveled to the San Francisco Bay. It had financial problems, but was finally completed in 1898. This meant that the people of California now had a competitive road.

Congress also passed the Thurman Act that required that the Central Pacific pay back its government loan, with 3% interest. This debt of about $60 million was settled completely by 1909.

In 1911, a California governor was elected whose single campaign promise was to kick the railroad out of politics. Hiram Johnson kept that promise with the help of the California lawmakers and the Railroad Commission.

Chapter Nine

The Big Four After the Golden Spike

Charlie Crocker

Charlie Crocker worked for a year after the Golden Spike, fine-tuning the railroad tracks and schedules. When this work was completed he became restless. Running the railroad was now a desk job and Crocker never cared to work behind a desk.

In 1871, Crocker decided to travel in Europe. He sold his part of the directorship to his partners. For the next two years, the Big Four became the Big Three. Then, in 1873, a financial panic swept the country. Even the Central Pacific was unable to make a large cash payment that a lender demanded. In New York City, Collis Huntington was worried. Crocker returned from Europe and asked Huntington for an installment of money the railroad owed him. Huntington explained the current problems and asked Crocker for money. Crocker agreed, and rejoined his associates. The Big Four were back together.

Crocker was concerned with things other than the railroad. His family wanted to build a mansion on Nob Hill in San Francisco. Crocker built a house so elaborate it was called "a delirium of a wood carver." It had a tower with a sweeping view

The Crocker house on the left. The spite fence is in the rear.

of San Francisco. In 1876, the Crockers held an expensive reception at the house to celebrate their twenty-fifth wedding anniversary. It was the talk of the town.

Crocker became the talk of the town in another way. A rich man, used to having his way, Crocker became irritated when his neighbor refused to sell him a lot that would give the Crocker mansion the full square city block it stood on. Mr. Yung, the owner of the lot, was an undertaker. His cottage had been there before Crocker's mansion, and he liked the view. Angry at Mr. Yung's refusal to sell, Crocker had a forty foot high "spite fence" built that surrounded Yung's cottage on three sides, entirely spoiling his view.

People gossiped about what Crocker had done. They climbed

Nob Hill in droves to see it. Newspaper editors and cartoonists poked fun. The fence came to be seen as "a symbol of the arrogance of wealth." A rally of the Workingmen's Party nearby started a small riot that led to fire and violence.

Yung finally sold Crocker the lot. But Crocker now often felt trapped inside his mansion. He longed to be away. He turned his Central Pacific business work over to his oldest son.

Restless, Charlie was on the move once again. He continued to build irrigation systems in the San Joaquin Valley. He supervised the building of a railroad resort hotel, Del Monte, on Monterey Bay. There he died in a diabetic coma on August 14, 1888.

Mark Hopkins

After the Golden Spike, Mark Hopkins became a familiar figure in Sacramento. Thin, with hunched shoulders, he leaned his 5' 10" height forward as he made his peculiar, slow stride to work and back. When he fell into deep thought, he would stroke his rather long, scraggly beard with a bony hand. He looked so much older than his age that people began to refer to him as "Uncle Mark." Calling him "Uncle" showed their fondness for him, and some would cross the street when they saw him just to say hello.

Hopkins and his wife Mary regretted never having children. But during the years the Central Pacific was under construction, fate brought a child into their life. In 1862, the Hopkinses heard about the plight of a widowed mother and hired her to help in their Sacramento house. They became very fond of her bright little son Timothy. Timothy stayed on with them when his mother married the gardener of Hopkins' vegetable farm and moved away. The Hopkins sent Timothy to school in Sacramento and San Francisco, and he was given a job with the railroad. He did very well and worked his way up to assistant treasurer.

By 1873, the Central Pacific had long been connecting Sacramento with San Francisco, and the headquarters was moved to the larger city. It made sense to move. Mary Hopkins disliked living in a rented house on Sutter Street when the Crockers and the Stanfords were making trips to Europe and building fine houses. She insisted they build a mansion, too, and her husband gave in. He himself had simple tastes and would have been forever happy in a small house.

Mary had her architects erect a wooden castle of gables, towers, steeples, and decoration that astounded the city with its fantastic silhouette. The house took some years to build because Mary kept making additions. Hopkins did not regret the wait. He wasn't anxious to live there, but he was glad to see Mary happy.

Mark's rheumatism worsened in the damp San Francisco climate and his gaunt figure grew more hunched. In March 1878, he decided to inspect the Southern Pacific route through Arizona, hoping the desert heat would make him feel better. On the trip he died unexpectedly as he napped in his railroad car.

Stanford and Hopkins built mansions on San Francisco's Nob Hill. Stanford's is on the left.

Leland Stanford

Jane and Leland Stanford moved to San Francisco in 1874 and built a mansion on two acres of Nob Hill. Stanford kept busy in other ways. He invested in a newfangled mechanism—the cable car, whose chain and links were buried in the street, allowing easy ascent of the steep hills. He also bought a 9,000 acre farm at Palo Alto where he bred and trained race horses, and financed an experiment of photographing horses in motion with a series of cameras lined up on a fence next to the track. He bought 55,000 acres in the northern Sacramento Valley and experimented with vineyards and wine-making.

The Stanfords had been childless for twenty years before their son Leland Jr. was born in 1868. He was the focus of his parent's lives. Leland Jr. took lessons in music, dancing, art, and French. Leland Jr. loved to learn and developed an interest in antique coins. He was also fascinated with mechanical things, especially anything related to railroads.

Before Leland Jr. entered Harvard in 1883, his father decided to go abroad. The Stanfords spent the summer in England, Germany, and France. They visited Vienna, Buda-Pest, Bucharest, and Constantinople.

Then Leland Jr. became sick in Athens and, because the weather was bad, the family sailed for Naples and continued to Rome. Leland Jr., however, grew sicker, and they hastened to Florence for a drier climate.

In Florence, Leland's sickness was diagnosed as typhoid fever. His body was wrapped in sheets dipped in ice-water. The street outside was covered with straw to deaden the noises. But

Leland Stanford left most of his fortune to the university named for his son.

Leland Stanford Jr.'s death at age fifteen devastated both of his parents.

nothing helped. Leland Jr. died on March 13, 1884, two months before his sixteenth birthday.

When the grief-stricken parents returned to California they wanted to memorialize their son. They considered building a museum or a technical school. Then, in 1886, the Stanfords announced that they were starting the Leland Stanford, Jr. University on their Palo Alto farm. They planned to leave their joint estate of $30 million to the university.

Leland Stanford was elected U.S. Senator in 1885. The Stanfords bought a house in Washington D. C., where they lived when Congress was in session.

But building the university was Stanford's first priority. They visited Johns Hopkins University, the Massachusetts

Institute of Technology, Cornell, and Harvard to talk with scholars. They declared that Stanford University would be a center of invention and research, co-educational and interdenominational. There would be no tuition. And there was to be no political control. The university opened in 1891.

On June 20, 1893, Leland Stanford died. His estate was "frozen" in what the law calls "probate" until all debts were paid. His share of what the Big Four owed the government for railroad loans was a huge amount. It looked as if Stanford University might have to close. Finally, a judge ruled that professors and staff could be considered personal servants of Mrs. Stanford and paid out of her money. Students no longer received free tuition, however.

Collis Huntington

Collis Huntington was always content to let others be in the spotlight. But after his friend Hopkins died in 1878, Huntington grumbled that he worked much harder than Crocker and Stanford. He expanded the Big Four's ownership of the Central Pacific and invested the group's money in other railroads, such as the Southern Pacific.

Acting for himself, Huntington bought the Chesapeake & Ohio Railroad and connected it to New Orleans by buying several small railroads and fixing them up. He became the first man to travel from the Atlantic coast to the Pacific coast on his own rails.

Huntington's business interests became a large and complex

empire. He worked long hours in his office in New York City behind the glass door that read simply *C. P. Huntington.*

Huntington's faithful wife Elizabeth died in October, 1883. The next July he married a young widow, Arabella Yarrington Worsham. Arabella was from Alabama, but she had become a real estate speculator in New York City where her first husband had been a small banker. Huntington adopted her son Archer, who loved history and became a Latin American scholar.

Arabella was very different from Elizabeth. She dressed fashionably and loved owning beautiful things and being the center of society. She persuaded Collis to build houses and buy paintings.

Though Arabella changed Huntington's life-style, he still enjoyed attending to business more than he enjoyed anything else. He was good at it. It had been Huntington's decision to become involved in the Central Pacific, and to bring in the others. This decision provided the basis for a life that would allow his intelligence, boldness, persistence, and energy to develop in a spectacular way. He became one of the most respected, and feared, businessmen of his time.

Collis Huntington had been exceptionally healthy all his life, and he was convinced he would live to 100, maybe longer. He was almost eighty when he awoke early one morning in August, 1900 and said, "I am very ill," and then died. The last of the Big Four was gone. But the railroad they built helped bind the United States together as one nation from the Atlantic to the Pacific Ocean.

Notes

Page 9: In 1836 there were only 100 miles of railroad and not more than ten steam locomotives in the United States.

Page 12: Henry R. Judah, Ted's father, was an Episcopalian priest in St. John's parish in Troy, New York. The Troy parish was interracial, which may in part account for Ted's strong anti-slavery views.

Page 14: In 1844 an extension of the Connecticut River Railroad brought it north to Greenfield. Five years later the line was extended to Brattleboro, Vermont.

Page 19: Mark Hopkins' father was a Methodist minister know for his strong abolitionist stand. Harriet Beecher Stowe based a character in *Uncle Tom's Cabin* on him.

Page 30: Elizabeth Huntington fought the fire of November 2, 1852 until she fainted from exhaustion. Collis left the burning building wrapped in a wet blanket.

Page 37: Anna did an exquisite pressing of the flowers and was able to identify almost everything: wild gillia, primrose, May weed, pink and white yarrows, wild potato, maiden hair, snapdragon, mountain lily, shooting star, buttercup, buckeye tree, wild larkspur of California, moss pink, wild coreopsis, Solomon seal, wild monkshood, nutmeg plant, wild rose, wild white lily. She added the leaves of coffee, magnolia, and wild cherry. Later she included oak moss from their residence in San Mateo. The album can be viewed at the Greenfield, Connecticut Historical Society.

Page 38: Asa Whitney tried to woo Congress for a land grant for his railroad again in 1848. By 1850, eighteen state legislatures had endorsed his plan and recommended it to Congress. Later, Whitney went to Great Britian in a vain attempt to interest Parliament in a trans-Canada railroad.

Page 60: Anna moved back to the old Pierce house to live with her aging parents and her brother Charles, who had been wounded in the Civil War. She wanted to always be identified with her beloved husband and made several trips back to California to visit their favorite places.

Page 70: Huntington once said this about the Big Four's relationship: "We were successful, we four, because of our teamwork. Each complemented the other in something the other lacked. There was Stanford, for instance, a man elected senator and governor, a man who loved to deal with people. He was a good lawyer. There was Mark Hopkins. He was a fine accountant and understood the value of everything. He was a thrifty man. Then, there was Crocker, the organizer, the executive, the driver of men."

Page 76: Thomas Durant was taken hostage near Piedmont, Wyoming by 300 angry Union Pacific workers demanding back pay which may have amounted to as much as $200,000. The Union Pacific was notorious for late wages. The Central Pacific paid regularly in gold and silver carried to the men by Charlie Crocker.

Timeline

1804   Lewis and Clark Expedition explores the territory between the Missouri River and the Pacific Ocean, making it clear that there is no transcontinental waterway.

1807   Robert Fulton's steam-powered boat successfully travels from New York City to Albany in 32 hours, averaging almost 5 miles per hour.

1813   Mark Hopkins born in Henderson, New York.

1817   Work begins on the Erie Canal to connect the Great Lakes with New York City via the Hudson River.

1821   Collis Potter Huntington born near Harwinton, Connecticut.

1822   Charles Crocker born in Troy, New York.

1824   Leland Stanford born in Watervliet, New York.

1825   The Erie Canal opens between Albany and Buffalo, New York. Barges pulled by mules slosh along at three miles per hour.

Steam-powered freight and passenger service begins on England's Stockton & Darlington, the world's first passenger railroad.

1826   Theodore Judah born in Bridgeport, Connecticut.

First railroad in the U.S. is the horse-drawn Quincy Tramway, running three miles between granite quarries at Quincy, Massachusetts and the Neponset River.

1830   First successful run of a steam-powered American locomotive, the *Tom Thumb*, built by Peter Cooper in Baltimore, Maryland. Its speed is 18 miles per hour.

1831   First American-built locomotive *Best Friend of Charleston* opens passenger service on the South Carolina Railroad between Charleston and Hamburg. It reaches a speed of 21 miles per hour.

       The Mohawk & Hudson Railroad begins a 16 mile operation between Albany and Schenectady, New York.

1834   The Renssalaer & Saratoga Railroad offers daily freight and passenger service from the Hudson River ferry terminal at Troy, New York to the foothills of the Adirondack Mountains.

1836   There are 100 miles of railroad track in the U.S. and about ten locomotives.

1847   Theodore Judah builds the Niagara Gorge Railroad and establishes his reputation.

1848   Discovery of gold at John Sutter's sawmill near Sacramento, California. Gold-fever sweeps the country.

1852   The first passenger train reaches Chicago via the Michigan Southern & Northern Indiana Railroad.

1853   U.S. Army engineers are designated to survey five possible railroad routes between the Mississippi Valley and the Pacific Ocean. Jefferson Davis, then U.S. Secretary of War, is in charge.

       Survey begins for a railroad connection west from Rock Island, Illinois to Council Bluffs, Iowa. Peter Dey and Grenville Dodge are the engineers for the Mississippi & Missouri Railroad.

1854   Theodore Judah begins work on the Sacramento Valley Railroad, the first in the West.

1855   The first locomotive in the West arrives by ship and is unloaded on the wharf at Sacramento for the Sacramento Valley Railroad.

1859   Hannibal & St. Joseph Railroad in the first to reach the upper Missouri River.

       The Railway Convention in San Francisco convened by the California Legislature supports the Central Route through Northern California and appoints Theodore Judah to take its recommendation to the U.S. Congress.

1860   The Pony Express completes its first ten-day run with mail between St. Joseph, Missouri and San Francisco, California. Theodore Judah and Daniel Strong discover the Donner Pass-Truckee River route as feasible for railroad construction over the Sierras.
Abraham Lincoln is elected President of the United States.

1861   The first shot of the Civil War is fired at Fort Sumter, South Carolina on April 12. On April 20, the Central Pacific Railroad is incorporated with Leland Stanford as President, Collis Huntington as Vice-President, Mark Hopkins as Treasurer, James Bailey as Secretary, and Theodore Judah as Chief Engineer.
In October the first telegraph message to San Francisco is completed, making the Pony Express obsolete.

1862   President Lincoln signs the Pacific Railroad Act on July 1.

1863   Ground broken for the Central Pacific Railroad on January 8. Theodore Judah dies November 2, in New York City, where he had traveled after quarreling with the Big Four. Samuel Montague replaces Judah as Chief Engineer for the Central Pacific.

1864   A second Railroad Act gives the transcontinental railroad more financial help.

1865   Charles Crocker begins hiring Chinese as laborers for the Central Pacific. The Civil War ends on April 9.

1867   The Summit Tunnel, through 1,659 feet of solid granite, is completed in the Sierras on May 3.

1869   On April 29 Charlie Crocker wins $10,000 when the Central Pacific crew lay 10 miles of track in one day.
May 10 is Golden Spike Day at Promontory, Utah. The last track is ceremoniously laid to complete the transcontinental railroad.

1871   Construction of the Southern Pacific Railroad begins in California to connect San Francisco with Southern California through the Central Valley, thus completing a southern route eastward to El Paso and New Orleans.

1878   Mark Hopkins dies near Yuma, Arizona.

1884   Consolidation of the Central Pacific and Southern Pacific
        Railroads.
1887   The Interstate Commerce Commission is created to deal with
        monopolistic practices by the railroads regarding freight rates,
        excessive political power, and unsound financing.
1888   Charles Crocker dies in Monterey, California.
1893   Leland Stanford dies in Palo Alto, California.
1898   The Santa Fe Railroad becomes the first transcontinental line
        to compete with the Southern Pacific in California.
1900   Collis Huntington dies in Pine Knot Camp, New York.
1906   The Hepburn Act allows the Interstate Commerce Commis-
        sion to set and regulate railroad rates. Theodore Roosevelt is
        President.

Bibliography

Bancroft, Hubert Howe. *History of the Life of Leland Stanford: A Character Study.* (Reprint) Oakland CA: Biobooks, 1952.

Brown, Dee. *Hear That Lonesome Whistle Blow: Railroads in the West.* New York: Holt, Rinehart, Winston, 1977.

Cleland, Robert G. *A History of California: The American Period.* New York: Macmillan, 1922.

Crawford, Alice. Interviews. She is retired historian and curator of the Greenfield Historical Society.

"Crocker, Charles." *Dictionary of American Biography.*

Dodge, Grenville, M. *How We Built the Union Pacific Railway.* Council Bluffs, Iowa: Monarch Press, 1910.

Harte, Bret. "What the Engines Said." *Best Loved Poems of the American West.* New York, Doubleday, 1980.

Howard, Robert West. *The Great Iron Trail: The Story of the First Transcontinental Railroad.* New York: G. P. Putnam, 1962.

"Huntington, Collis Potter." *Dictionary of American Biography.*

Jones, Helen Hinckley. *Rails from the West: A Biography of Theodore D. Judah.* San Marino, California: Golden West Books, 1969.

Jones, Irmarie. "Mrs. Judah Told of Pioneer Days." *Greenfield Recorder* 8 May, 1969.

Judah, Anna Pierce. *Anna Judah Papers.* University of California Bancroft Library, Berkeley. C-D 800, folio 3 on Microfilm. 1889.

Judah, Theodore Dehone. "Narrative of Journey." Unpublished manuscript. Pierce Family Collection.

"Judah, Theodore Dehone." *Dictionary of American Biography.*

Kellogg, Lucy Cutler. *Historic Greenfield.* Greenfield, Massachusetts: Greenfield, Massachusetts, Historical Society, 1926.

Kraus, George. *High Road to Promontory: Building the Central Pacific (now the Southern Pacific) across the High Sierra.* Palo Alto, California, 1969.

Lavender, David. *The Great Persuader.* New York: Doubleday, 1970.

Lewis, Oscar. *The Big Four.* New York: Knopf, 1966.

McCague, James. *Moguls and Iron Men.* New York: Harper and Row,1964.

Pierce Stephen. Judah Genealogy. Greenfield Historical Society files.

Reid, Gerald F. *150 Years: Heritage Bank of Greenfield and Amherst, Massachusetts.* Northampton, Massachusetts: Benjamin, 1984.

Senior, John A. "Because Area Man Dreamed, the RRs Joined." *Greenfield Recorder* 8 May 1969:7.

"Stanford, Leland." *Dictionary of American Biography.*

Thompson, Francis M. *History of Greenfield.* Greenfield, MA: T. Morey & Sons, 1904.

Titus, Benair. Interviews. She is the collateral cousin of Anna Pierce Judah and Gladys Pierce, and the holder of the Pierce Family Collection of papers, photos, and artifacts.

Weeks, W. Leon. *A Walking Tour of Downtown Historic District: Greenfield, Massachusetts.* Greenfield Heritage Trail Committee: pamphlet, undated 1980s.

Williams, John Hoyt. *A Great and Shining Road: The Epic Story of the Transcontinental Railroad.* New York: Times Books, 1988.

Index